.YOU'RE.
AMAZING

HOW TO CAST OFF SELF-DOUBT AND EMBRACE YOUR INNER BRILLIANCE

DEBBI MARCO

summersdale

YOU'RE AMAZING

An Hachette UK Company
www.hachette.co.uk

Summersdale Publishers Ltd
Part of Octopus Publishing Group Limited
Carmelite House
50 Victoria Embankment
LONDON
EC4Y 0DZ
UK

www.summersdale.com

Printed and bound in China

ISBN: 978-1-78783-573-3

Substantial discounts on bulk quantities of Summersdale books are available to corporations, professional associations and other organizations. For details contact general enquiries: telephone: +44 (0) 1243 771107 or email: enquiries@summersdale.com.

CONTENTS

INTRODUCTION

Have you ever thought that "amazing" was for other people and not for you? Perhaps you look at people like Michelle Obama or David Attenborough and think you could never achieve everything they have. Or maybe it's a work colleague or sibling who's set the bar high. Being amazing is such a personal thing and what it means for your life is really up to you. It could mean finding success in work, love or friendship, an achievement in sport or mastering a musical instrument. Perhaps it's simply following your heart to make a long-held dream come true. But there is

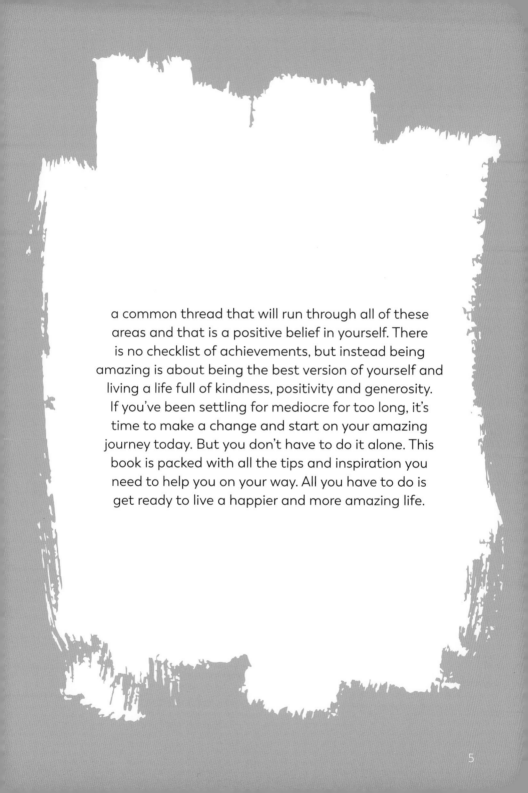

a common thread that will run through all of these areas and that is a positive belief in yourself. There is no checklist of achievements, but instead being amazing is about being the best version of yourself and living a life full of kindness, positivity and generosity. If you've been settling for mediocre for too long, it's time to make a change and start on your amazing journey today. But you don't have to do it alone. This book is packed with all the tips and inspiration you need to help you on your way. All you have to do is get ready to live a happier and more amazing life.

CHAPTER ONE:
WHAT IS AMAZING?

Think of the feeling you have when you see a beautiful sunset, or receive a bear hug from your loved one that fills you with joy and happiness. The feeling when you complete a long run or make a cake that doesn't sink in the middle. All of these things, big and small, add up to amazing. The feeling of "amazing" can be wrapped up in success, human connections, time out and tiny achievements. Only you know what sort of amazing life you're seeking, so make a commitment to yourself to find out. On the way try to start each day with a positive attitude. Take the time to appreciate the little things that make every day count. Spread joy and kindness to others – what could be more amazing than that?

WEAR A CROWN OF KINDNESS

Being kind is the most worthwhile thing you can do with your time. It will cost you nothing, but it will make you feel as though you're the richest person around. If you don't believe me, then try it. Commit to one act of kindness each day and see how you feel after a week or two. It could be anything from paying someone a compliment, buying a coffee for the person in the queue behind you or going out of your way to chat to someone who seems lonely. Kindness is so powerful it will flow in both directions, making both you and the recipient feel better.

You only live once, but if you do it right, once is enough.

Mae West

PERFECT YOUR POSITIVITY

There's one sure-fire way to set you on the path to an amazing life – remaining positive. Of course, it's not as easy as simply *wanting* to always look on the bright side. Think of positivity as a muscle that needs to be exercised regularly; the more you can think and act in a positive way, the easier it will get and the more ways you will find to be positive. Start small: write down three good things that have happened to you at the end of each day. These can be as simple as getting a seat on the train to work or finding no queue in the coffee shop. As you start to get better at spotting the good things that happen each day, you'll feel stronger when bad things happen. Soon you should be able to turn around a not-so-good situation and find the silver lining to any dark cloud that appears on the horizon. The more positive things you say and think, the better you will feel. The more finding positivity becomes your default setting, the happier and more amazing your life will be.

THE GIFT OF GIVING

It's a cliché to say that giving often feels better than receiving, but that's because it's true. Don't worry – this doesn't mean you have to become a year-round Santa Claus, giving presents to everyone you meet. Instead it means being generous with the things you already have, such as your time, your humour and your smile. If someone looks as though they need a chat, invite them to lunch or for a coffee. Often just a 10-minute conversation can lift a person's mood. Even smiling at the cashier in the supermarket or letting a car out in a traffic jam can be an act of generosity. Try to "give" one thing each day and you'll soon find you feel much richer than before.

You don't
have to be

perfect

to be

amazing

I avoid looking forward or backward, and try to keep looking upward.

CHARLOTTE BRONTË

TURN YOUR FROWN UPSIDE DOWN

Negative thoughts tend to work like a black hole that sucks in everything around it, but with a bit of practice you can turn your negative thoughts into positive ones. The first step is to notice when you're having a negative thought or reaction to something. After you notice, try to apply one positive thought to each negative one, then build up to two or three positive thoughts for each negative one. You'll soon get in the habit of replacing your thoughts with positive ones and you'll find life takes on a whole different feel.

RIDE THE WAVE OF ENTHUSIASM

Do you know someone who just has so much energy and enthusiasm for life they seem to lift up everyone around them? Well, there's no reason why you can't be that person. Crank up your enthusiasm levels by saying yes to as many opportunities as possible and then give them your all. Make sure you don't burn out, but by changing your immediate reaction to "let's do this!" you'll be opening yourself up to a plethora of positive experiences. If you're unsure where to start, try spending time with an enthusiastic buddy and allow yourself to be swept along by their energy. Enthusiasm is infectious and it will pretty soon become a part of your life if you let it. When you tackle life with this attitude, you'll soon view even the most stressful and frustrating tasks as challenging instead of troublesome.

UNLEASH THE AMAZINGNESS INSIDE

BUILD YOURSELF UP

We are so used to telling ourselves we are a certain way or we can't do something, that we never stop to think about whether our narrative is true or not. Try turning things around by being your own cheerleader. Even if you're not sure you can succeed, tell yourself you can and then give it a try. Perhaps you don't think you'd be good at baking or dancing or rock climbing. Tell yourself you can do it and then go ahead and give it a go. There's a good chance you'll be surprised by the results – and if you're not, you'll be proud of yourself for trying.

CHANGE
WILL NOT COME
IF WE WAIT
FOR SOME
OTHER PERSON
OR SOME
OTHER TIME.

WE ARE
THE ONES
WE'VE BEEN
WAITING FOR.
WE ARE
THE CHANGE
THAT WE SEEK.

BARACK OBAMA

SPREAD YOUR AMAZINGNESS

You'll soon see that how you behave is reflected back in the world around you. This has never been truer than when it comes to those closest to you. If you start to be an amazing partner and friend, you'll soon find that the special people in your life will become amazing too. Pay compliments, make cups of tea for the team, sort a busy friend's laundry – it will all help spread the amazing and you'll start to see it reflected back to you. Even something small, such as trying not to be grumpy in the morning, can change your daily life from fraught to fantastic.

AMAZE YOUR FRIENDS

Don't limit your amazingness to those you see regularly. Long-distance friends will benefit from your new outlook on life too. A simple text, email or postcard with an inspirational message (copy one from the pages of this book if you like) will uplift them and set them on track to feel better, be positive, increase their self-belief and get on the path to being amazing. It also lets them know you are thinking of them – and feeling cherished will give anyone a lift.

BE A ROLE MODEL

It's easy to look to the Greta Thunbergs of this world and think you could never be so inspirational. But you don't have to be a teenage climate change campaigner to make your mark. Focus your attention a bit closer to home and see if there is someone in your life you could inspire. Perhaps there is an intern at work who could do with a bit of mentoring or career advice. It doesn't matter if you're not top of your game, anyone starting out will appreciate the experience of another person in their field. Or maybe you could inspire a sibling or a child to put in that extra effort, train for a big event or even just approach life with a great attitude. It may not feel like you're changing the world, but simply being happy, polite and considerate whenever you can will make you a great role model for all those around you – and will help make your life better too.

GIVE YOURSELF CREDIT FOR
OVERCOMING THINGS –

YOU MADE
IT THIS FAR!

PAY IT FORWARD

Imagine a line of dominoes all standing up straight.
When you push one, it falls down, knocking over the next
one in the process. Little nuggets of kindness, positivity
and amazingness can work in the same way. If you do
something nice for someone, like giving up your seat on
a crowded bus, holding the door open or letting someone
go in front of you in the supermarket queue, chances
are that person will feel buoyed up and will go on to
do something nice for someone else, who in turn will
also pay it forward, transforming an otherwise average
day into one filled with kindness and connection.

The more you praise and celebrate your life, the more there is in life to celebrate.

OPRAH WINFREY

You did not wake up today to be mediocre

MAKE YOURSELF A MAGNET

It's true that like attracts like, so with that in mind think about what and who you would like to surround yourself with. It might help you to write down a list of words or things that you would like more of in your life, to help you focus. If you can apply a "glass half full" attitude to most things in life, it's likely you'll attract other people who have a positive outlook too. And you'll find that more good things will happen to you – not only because you will be able to find the positive in any situation, but also because your new view on life will encourage you to seek these things out. When you approach life with a sunny, positive attitude, you'll be open to new opportunities, which will make your life feel full of excitement and happiness. By being a fun-loving, generous and positive person you will be a magnet for people who also want to live their life in the way you do.

FAKE IT TILL YOU MAKE IT

Of course, some days you will feel low and not very amazing at all. It's okay to feel this way, but the important thing is not to let these feelings of despair and depression overwhelm you. Set yourself a time to deal with any unhappy feelings, then paint a smile on your face and do your best to pretend to feel positive and happy. It might not work straight away, but you'll find saying positive things and acting in a positive and happy way will soon penetrate your inner feelings, and before you know it life will start to feel a little bit better again.

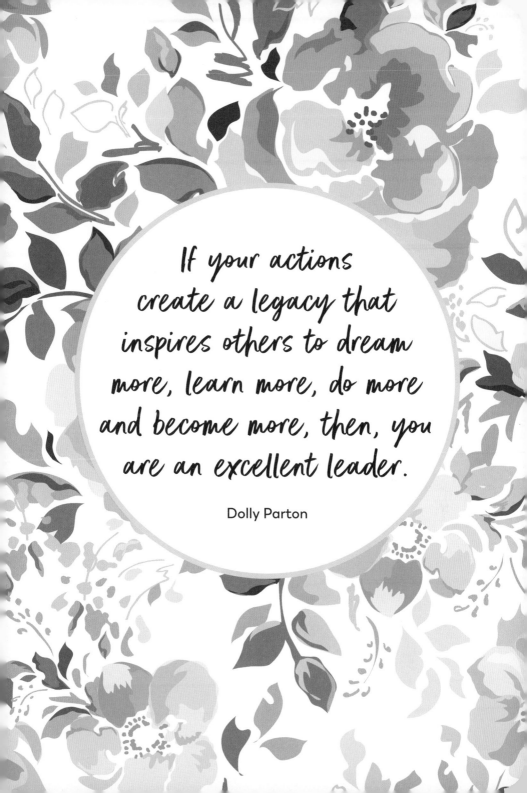

If your actions create a legacy that inspires others to dream more, learn more, do more and become more, then, you are an excellent leader.

Dolly Parton

Believe in
yourself
so strongly
that the world
can't help but
believe
in you too

OPEN YOUR MIND

No one has all the answers, which is why it's great to be inspired by others. Look to those around you to see how they live an amazing life. Maybe your work colleague volunteers once a month or your friend has an elderly neighbour she looks out for. Make a commitment to try something new each week or do something differently to how you usually do it. You never know, you might like it!

FLIP FAILURE AROUND

Most people think of failure as a negative thing, but if you look at it the right way it could be the best thing that ever happened to you. For a start, if you don't fail it means you're not trying anything new – which is pretty boring! Also, every time you fail, it's a learning experience and one that will help you grow stronger and smarter. As children we failed all the time, but we didn't give up, we got up and kept going. Otherwise, how else would we have learned to ride a bike or swim or be able to do our multiplication tables? Instead of using the word "failing", replace it with "learning". Each time you try something new, list the things you have learned. You'll soon see that, successful or not, you are moving forward and growing as a person.

IT DOES NOT MATTER HOW SLOWLY YOU GO, AS LONG AS YOU DO NOT STOP.

CONFUCIUS

STAND UP FOR OTHERS

Being an amazing person is not just about self-improvement. It also involves doing things for other people and that includes having the courage to speak out on behalf of others. This can be something big such as calling out racism or sexism, or it can be helping someone get their voice heard in a meeting or making sure a colleague receives credit for a great idea. If you're constantly on the lookout for how you can speak up for others, you'll also find it easier to stand up for yourself. When you practise speaking out, it will become habit-forming and soon you won't think twice about doing the right thing.

GIVE YOURSELF PERMISSION TO LIVE A BIG LIFE.

STEP INTO WHO YOU ARE MEANT TO BE.

STOP PLAYING SMALL.

YOU ARE MEANT FOR GREATER THINGS.

WHEN THE GOING GETS TOUGH...

It can be easy to slump into a grump when things don't go your way, but don't forget why you are trying to change your life to be more amazing. You know deep down that by making positive steps toward kindness, generosity and optimism, you have the power to change your life and the lives of those around you. That doesn't mean it will be easy, but keep trying as it will be worth it in the end.

Pearls

don't lie on the seashore. If you want one, you must dive for it.

Proverb

PRACTISE PATIENCE

Changing your behaviour and mindset is never easy, so it's important that you are kind to yourself as you increase the amazing in your life. Don't worry if you trip up, can't sustain your positive thinking or don't manage to meet any of the targets you set yourself. We all have bad days, weeks and even months. The important thing is to keep on trying. Giving up is the only thing you should berate yourself for – and if you're annoyed then you haven't quite given up yet! The same is true for others around you. Try to be tolerant and kind when they make a mistake – remember failing is just an opportunity to learn. If you're determined to change, then you will. It will take hard work, failures and a few false starts, but with a focused mind you'll get there eventually.

Today
is your day
to be
amazing

TAKE SOME TIME OUT

Practise some self-care such as mindfulness or yoga. By doing this regularly you should feel refreshed and ready to face the day ahead. If you try to take a few minutes daily to recalibrate, it will give you the energy and strength to keep pursuing your goal of being even more amazing.

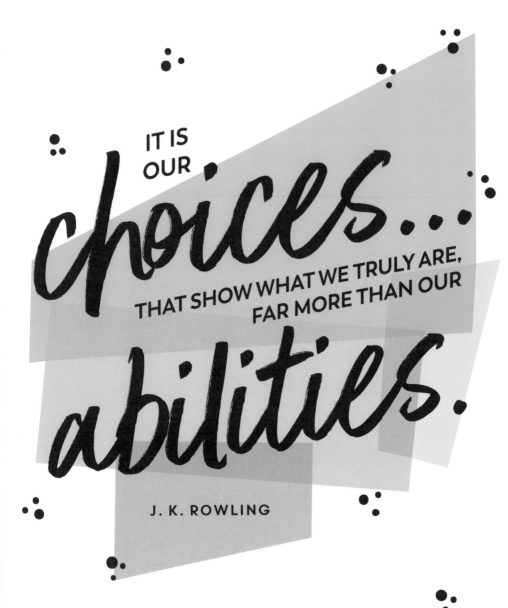

IT IS OUR *choices...* THAT SHOW WHAT WE TRULY ARE, FAR MORE THAN OUR *abilities.*

J. K. ROWLING

48

CHAPTER TWO:

EMBRACE AMAZING

It can feel slightly overwhelming to decide to change your life, but you are already amazing in so many ways – you probably just don't realize it yet. To be amazing can often simply be a matter of recognizing what already exists in your life and then building on those elements. Think about what makes you special and different and look at ways to expand these parts of your personality. It is also helpful to discover and address any less-than-helpful habits that will get in your way. You are the author of your own life, so get ready to create a really special happy ending for yourself while keeping hold of everything that is already amazing in your life.

DON'T GO CHASING UNICORNS

You might have fallen into the trap of thinking that to be amazing is to be perfect, but I've got some news for you: nothing and no one is ever perfect. Perfection doesn't really exist and the desire to live a perfect life can actually be a very negative one. You can waste a lot of your energy chasing perfection because it's a goal that you will never reach – and it could potentially make you very unhappy and unhealthy if you keep trying to get to something that doesn't exist. Release yourself from the myth that you need to be perfect and start to look at what will really make you happy.

Be a pineapple:
stand tall, wear a crown
and be sweet
on the inside

TRY NOT TO COMPARE

It is one thing to be inspired by those around you and another to compare yourself with others. For a start, you will never know what is happening behind the scenes with any individual and how many struggles and false starts they have overcome to get where they are. And also, so what? You are your own person, with your own goals, life and journey, so don't compare how far you've come and where you are going with anyone else. If there is a particular individual who has a negative influence on your mood, try to limit your interaction with them. Mute them in your social media channels and try to avoid them socially if you can. Think about what it is that is making you compare yourself with them. Do they seem more successful or happier than you? Can you figure out why you are feeling this way? Don't forget there is plenty of success to go around, and just because one individual seems to have a cupful it doesn't mean there isn't enough left for you. Don't waste energy thinking badly of them or yourself, instead focus on how you can reach your goals.

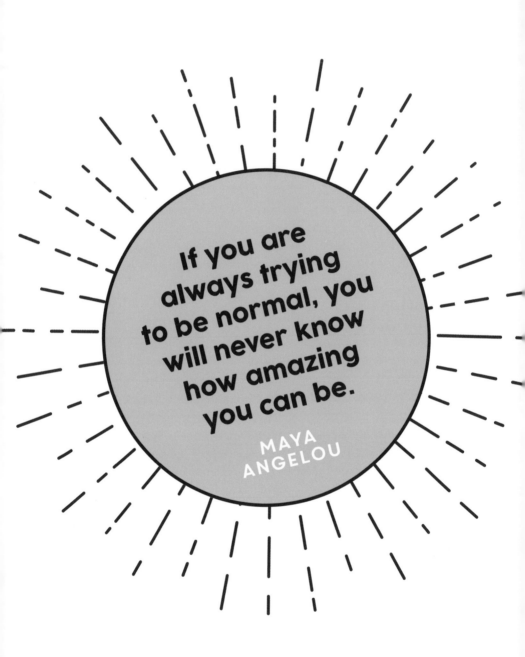

If you are always trying to be normal, you will never know how amazing you can be.

MAYA ANGELOU

Don't miss out on something AMAZING just because it could also be DIFFICULT

FIND A MENTOR

Whether you want to get better at work presentations, improve your health and fitness, get a handle on your anxiety or be a better parent or partner, find someone who can help. This could be a formal mentor at work or a therapist or trainer, but you could also invite a friend or colleague for coffee and ask for a chat. If you share your worries and ask for advice, people are usually happy to help. A different perspective and opinion could help you turn things around, transforming your problem into a positive opportunity.

We are what we believe we are.

C. S. LEWIS

EMBRACE WHO YOU ARE

You are great. No, really, you are! And if you want to live an amazing life, you need to start believing it. You may feel that you have faults, but this shouldn't stop you from embracing yourself exactly as you are. Just because you're trying to become a better person, it doesn't mean you're not a great individual right now. It's really important to accept and love yourself because, to move forward and grow as individual, you need a steady and safe platform much like the foundations of a building. You need to work on making these foundations as strong as possible and figure out all the reasons you are great. Maybe you volunteer for a charity each month, or you always make the tea at work or bring a friend flowers if they are feeling down. Think of all the things that make you unique and celebrate them. Once you've got those established, only then can you start to move forward and make improvements.

The sooner you start *believing* in yourself, the sooner you'll see *results*

CREATE CONFIDENCE

We all know someone who doesn't hesitate to grab the karaoke mic, won't break a sweat in an important presentation and has no problem captaining everything from the pub quiz team to the work sports team. It's easy to imagine they were born that way, but it is more likely that they are just used to stepping forward and volunteering. As with many things that scare us, the thought is often worse than the reality. Commit to doing one thing each month that takes you out of your comfort zone. It could be speaking up, joining a club or learning a new skill. You'll soon notice your confidence growing.

I LEARNED THAT **COURAGE** WAS NOT THE ABSENCE OF FEAR, BUT THE **TRIUMPH** OVER IT.

THE BRAVE MAN IS NOT HE WHO DOES NOT FEEL AFRAID, BUT HE WHO CONQUERS THAT FEAR.

NELSON MANDELA

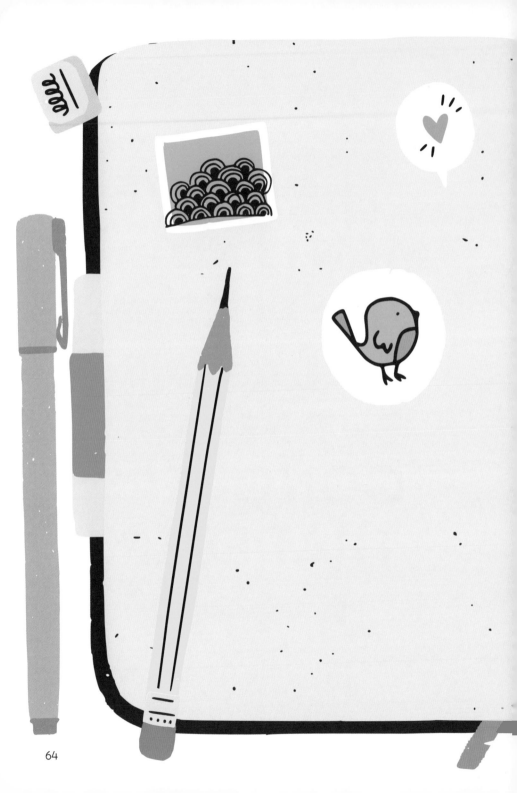

MAKE "AMAZING" WORK FOR YOU

Different things make different people happy and it's up to you to choose your own path. For some it might be connecting socially with those around them, while for others it could be learning a new skill or overcoming life-long fears. However you choose to make your life amazing, the most important thing is to recognize how you can achieve it. Sometimes a mood board covered with images of all the things you hope to do will help. Other people find it useful to work with someone they are close to, so they have a cheerleader to encourage them and keep them on track. If you're struggling to make a start, set yourself small, easily achievable goals, such as saying one kind thing a day or learning a new skill. Keep a journal so you can track your progress, write down positive thoughts and celebrate your successes.

HALFWAY TO AMAZING

You're already a pretty amazing person. However, there are probably a few things in your life that are holding you back and, in order to sort them out, you need to figure out what they are. Start by noting down all the good things about yourself, write a list or doodle some pictures to show what you really like about yourself. Ask a close friend for help if you're struggling to think of things. Then have a look at how you can build on those. Perhaps you can turn your baking skills into a fundraising opportunity or maybe your skills at work can be used to set up a training course to help others. The more you give, the more you'll get back and the richer your life will feel.

Forget the mistake and remember the lesson

WHAT MAKES YOU DIFFERENT OR WEIRD, THAT'S YOUR *strength.*

MERYL STREEP

STRIVE TO IMPROVE

List three things about yourself that you'd like to improve and start to brainstorm how you can make one of these changes. Begin by getting a large piece of paper and writing something you would like to improve in the middle, then work on filling the rest of the space with all the solutions to how you can make that happen. You should be feeling pretty empowered by the end of the session. Pick a couple of ideas that feel easy to achieve, then go ahead and put them into action.

CREATE TIME FOR YOURSELF

When you make yourself the star of your own life, you will feel more centred and grounded, living your life how you truly want. This doesn't mean being selfish, it's about finding happiness by really looking at what makes you happy and following that path. Make a point of spending a period of time each week on pursuing your dream. I'm not talking about becoming a Hollywood star, but something like training for a marathon, learning a new skill such as pottery or even volunteering with a local charity. Or perhaps you want to write a book but never have enough time. By setting aside a few hours a week to truly focus on yourself you will unleash all your amazing potential.

YOUR ONLY OBLIGATION IN LIFE IS TO BE YOURSELF

SMASH IT LIKE STORMZY

British rapper Stormzy is a role model to anyone who wants to follow their dream. He dropped out of college to follow his music career and ignored all the naysayers who said he would never make it without a manager and record label. Instead he focused on what he could do and got all his friends together to film a music video in a car park. The song, "Shut Up", sold more than half a million copies and Stormzy became one of the biggest UK rappers. Despite international fame, he still raps about how much he loves his mum and his goal is to inspire those who want to follow in his footsteps. He tells young black men who see him as a role model: "You can do this. You're better than anyone's ever told you that you are." Stormzy is an example to us all: if you want it badly enough, go out and get it.

The things in life which don't go to plan are usually more important, more formative, in the long run, than the things that do.

Maggie O'Farrell

Celebrate your strength

YOU ARE PERFECTLY
CAST IN YOUR LIFE.
I CAN'T IMAGINE ANYONE
BUT YOU IN THE ROLE.

LIN-MANUEL MIRANDA

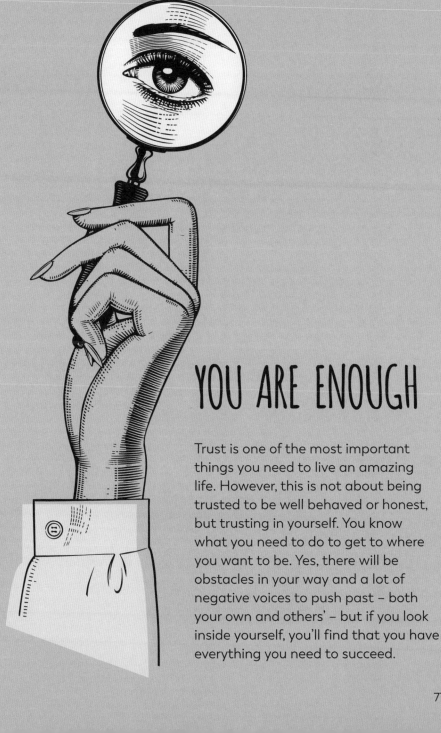

YOU ARE ENOUGH

Trust is one of the most important things you need to live an amazing life. However, this is not about being trusted to be well behaved or honest, but trusting in yourself. You know what you need to do to get to where you want to be. Yes, there will be obstacles in your way and a lot of negative voices to push past – both your own and others' – but if you look inside yourself, you'll find that you have everything you need to succeed.

STOP HATING YOURSELF FOR EVERYTHING YOU AREN'T

AND START LOVING YOURSELF FOR EVERYTHING YOU ARE

Life is inherently risky.
There is only one big risk you
should avoid at all costs and that
is the risk of doing nothing.

**DENIS
WAITLEY**

TAKE A GOOD LOOK AT YOURSELF

Find a mirror where you can see your whole face. Speaking aloud, start to say positive things about yourself. Say aloud your positive qualities, such as your kindness or patience. Tell yourself examples of when you have done kind things for other people. Come up with as many things as possible. Make a commitment to return to your mirror the following week with even more positives. Don't be afraid to say anything, however small or insignificant it may seem. You'll quickly see that every good, brave and kind thing you do adds up to amazing pretty quickly!

MAKE YOUR MARK, LIKE MALALA

When the Taliban forbade girls from going to school, Pakistani schoolgirl Malala Yousafzai took a stand. She wrote online that education was power for women and the reason the Taliban was closing girls' schools was because they didn't want women to be powerful. This brave stand put Malala directly in the firing line, literally, and a few days later she was shot by the Taliban. Miraculously she survived and went on to make a full recovery and became the youngest person ever to receive the Nobel Peace Prize. So even if you're feeling small, remember that standing up for what you believe in can change your life and the lives of those around you. You're never too young or insignificant to make a change.

Revel in your own amazingness!

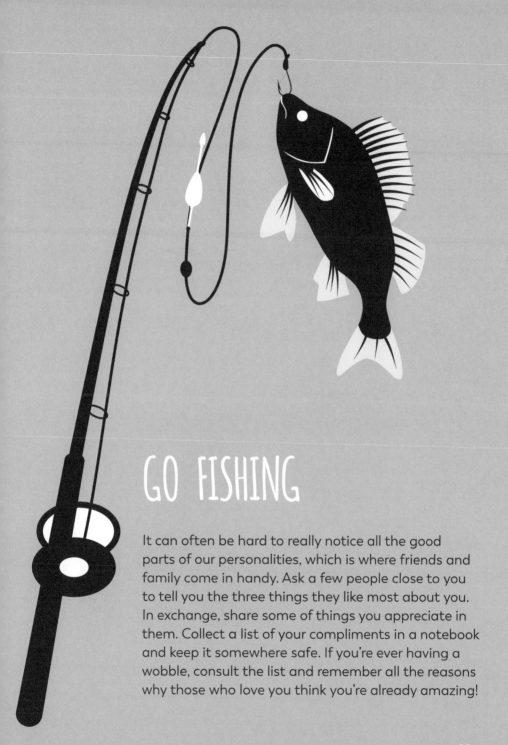

GO FISHING

It can often be hard to really notice all the good parts of our personalities, which is where friends and family come in handy. Ask a few people close to you to tell you the three things they like most about you. In exchange, share some of things you appreciate in them. Collect a list of your compliments in a notebook and keep it somewhere safe. If you're ever having a wobble, consult the list and remember all the reasons why those who love you think you're already amazing!

All our dreams can come true if we have the courage to pursue them.

Walt Disney

CHAPTER THREE:

EVERYDAY AMAZING

You might be surprised at how amazing you can be when you take the time to really focus on it. Pay a compliment to a stranger, take the time to check on your neighbour and give yourself the space you need to pursue your dreams. These are just some of the things you can do to keep on living an amazing life. Don't be overwhelmed or disappointed if you're not amazing each and every day. Remember, there's no sprint to the finish or prize for first place. View your amazing life as a gentle stroll where you take the time to appreciate all the little things around you.

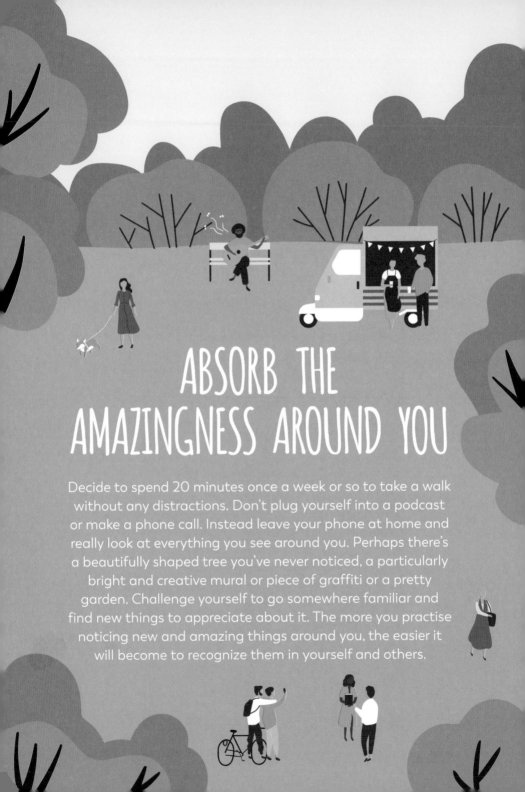

ABSORB THE AMAZINGNESS AROUND YOU

Decide to spend 20 minutes once a week or so to take a walk without any distractions. Don't plug yourself into a podcast or make a phone call. Instead leave your phone at home and really look at everything you see around you. Perhaps there's a beautifully shaped tree you've never noticed, a particularly bright and creative mural or piece of graffiti or a pretty garden. Challenge yourself to go somewhere familiar and find new things to appreciate about it. The more you practise noticing new and amazing things around you, the easier it will become to recognize them in yourself and others.

The best
preparation for
tomorrow
is doing
your best
today

DON'T BE TOO TIMID AND SQUEAMISH ABOUT YOUR ACTIONS.

ALL LIFE IS AN EXPERIMENT.

THE MORE EXPERIMENTS YOU MAKE THE BETTER.

RALPH WALDO EMERSON

WALK IN SOMEONE ELSE'S SHOES

It can be hard to feel amazing if someone is unkind to you. It might be someone you know – such as a friend or maybe a stranger or a work colleague – who has upset you. Don't worry, it's easy to get upset if you have been criticized or spoken to unfairly, but don't let it dull your sparkle. Instead, rewrite the incident from a different point of view. If a driver shouted at you from their car, consider they might have been rushing to hospital to visit a sick relative. Or if a work colleague was critical of your report, think about the pressure they may be under. By viewing others with compassion, you can take the sting out of their words and treat them with kindness, while keeping your amazingness intact.

When you feel like quitting, tell yourself: the story doesn't end this way

If you're offered a
seat on a rocket
ship, don't ask what
seat! Just get on.

SHERYL SANDBERG

NEVER GIVE UP ON YOURSELF - NO MATTER WHAT!

LEAP ANY HURDLE

When British Paralympian Jonnie Peacock was five he nearly lost his life to meningitis, but thankfully he only lost his leg. Thanks to his mum's "you can do anything" attitude and his own perseverance, Jonnie started athletics training at the age of 15 and went on to become a gold medallist and world record breaker in the T44 100m. But he is clear that his success comes from his personal determination, saying: "I don't feel pressure from anywhere else, I put that pressure on myself." Jonnie shows us that it's not the obstacles you face but how you tackle them that will move you forward in your goals.

I never dreamed about success. I worked for it.

ESTÉE LAUDER

TUNE OUT THE TOXICS

It's not easy to avoid everyone who is negative in your life, but learning how to dodge negative comments can only be a good thing. It might be a colleague or family member who is putting you down or knocking your goals, but don't let them. Avoid talking about certain topics with your family if possible or shut down your colleague's criticism by saying "thank you for your opinion" and move swiftly to a different subject.

MAKE A PLAN

People don't wake up one morning able to run a marathon or climb a mountain. They don't just become CEOs or skilled artists. All of those people who have achieved something in their life started in the same place – at the beginning and with a goal in mind. Pick just one thing you'd like to achieve in the next few months. Give yourself a rough timescale and then work out how you're going to achieve your goal. Write down the individual steps you'll need to take, what advice, support and resources you'll need and where you'll find those. Give yourself mini goals each week so you can keep on track and stay on top of your goal. Even if you need a little extra time or need to rethink a few things, you'll have learned so much in planning and achieving goals.

DO WHAT MAKES YOU HAPPY

When was the last time you put yourself first? We have so many commitments to family, work and friends that it can be hard create a space for ourselves, but it's important that you do. This could involve choosing to see the film you want to watch or eating at your favourite restaurant, or maybe just taking half an hour to read a book. Whatever it is that you would like to do, make sure you find some time and space to do it. You'll be amazed how it can re-energize you and make you feel a whole lot more amazing.

LISTEN TO THE QUIET VOICE WITHIN; DON'T LET THE LOUD ONE ALWAYS GET YOUR ATTENTION

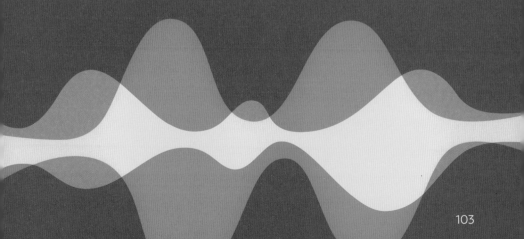

Don't judge each day by the harvest you reap but by the seeds that you plant.

Robert Louis Stevenson

CELEBRATE YOUR VICTORIES

When you cross the finish line or hit your targets it's easy to give yourself a high five. But there are plenty of smaller wins along the way that deserve a celebration too. They can be as small as making it to work on time for a week or remembering your reusable coffee cup every day. It could be remembering to phone your mum once a week or not beating yourself up because you deviated from your healthy eating plan by enjoying a slice of cake. Whatever it is, try to celebrate at least one win a day. Go ahead – give yourself a high five!

TAKE A STAND LIKE MEGAN RAPINOE

Megan Rapinoe is one of the most famous soccer players in the world, and she isn't afraid to speak her mind and use her public position to help others. Not only is she the first player of any gender to score directly from a corner in the Olympic Games, but she matches her skills on the pitch with her commitment to activism off it. In 2016 she knelt when the American national anthem was played to show solidarity for fellow sportsman Colin Kaepernick to protest against racial injustice and minority oppression. Rapinoe has openly spoken out against Donald Trump and described herself as "a walking protest" when she said she would refuse to go to the White House should her team win the World Cup (which it did in 2019). She said: "I would encourage my teammates to think hard about lending that platform or having that co-opted by an administration that doesn't feel the same way and doesn't fight for the same things we fight for." It's not easy to do the right thing, but sometimes it is the only option.

YOU'LL BE AMAZED AT WHAT YOU ATTRACT

AFTER YOU START BELIEVING IN WHAT YOU DESERVE

FOCUS ON THE JOURNEY

It's easy to become so focused on your goal and what you want to achieve in life that you forget to enjoy the journey to get there. And often that's the part that takes the longest. It's great to have a goal, but don't sacrifice your happiness to achieve it. Keep an eye on your day-to-day happiness and make sure you are still enjoying life. Sometimes goals come at a great cost, so make sure that what you're aiming for is worth it.

Your success is
not final - nor is
your failure.

**GEORGE
MATTHEW ADAMS**

TAKE A BACK SEAT

While it's important to do things to make yourself happy,
thinking of others is a key part of living an amazing life.
Consider the needs of those around you and make them
feel important. Pick one day a week to spoil someone close
to you: let them choose what you watch on Netflix or sit in
the comfiest spot on the sofa. Cook dinner or do the food
shopping if you don't usually, or simply surprise them with
a hug and tell them all the reasons they're amazing.

Difficult roads often lead to beautiful destinations

DON'T BE OVERWHELMED

Life is busy and it can often feel like you're drowning under a sea of things to do. It's completely normal to feel like it's all getting out of control, but once you have noticed that it has it's time to act. Write down everything that is getting on top of you and split the list into sections. Work out what is important and what can slide for this month or be passed on to someone else. Once you have a to-do list work out some deadlines and priorities. Breaking down your chores into manageable chunks will make you feel a whole lot better. Don't forget to include some downtime for yourself on your list otherwise you'll be back to square one before you know it.

The bad news is
news is
time flies.
The good news
is you're the
pilot.

MICHAEL ALTSHULER

LIVE A LIFE OF PASSION

A good job, stable relationship and nice home may feel like you're ticking all the boxes, but what if you're still feeling as if something is missing? Listen to what your inner voice is saying and try to make a change. If you're working a 9-to-5 office job but you've always dreamed of being a singer, why not seek out an open mic night? If you've always lived in the same town, you could make plans to travel somewhere you've always dreamed of. It might not be easy but if you start working on your goals now, you'll find life looks very different in a year or two.

ROLL THE DICE

Sometimes you need someone or something to force your hand to make a change. Big changes can often be beyond our control, such as redundancy or ill health, but what if you could make a life change for yourself without waiting for something to happen? Write down a list of six things you've always wanted to do. These could be travelling, training for a new career or starting a hobby you've never been brave enough to try before. Number your list, roll a dice and then commit to achieving whichever goal comes up.

It doesn't matter where you are coming from. All that matters is where you are going.

Brian Tracy

JAR OF SWEETNESS

Every day think of three things you have been grateful for that day. Write them on scraps of paper that you can fold and put in a jar. These can be anything from getting a lie-in, someone making you a cup of tea or even simply not burning your toast in the morning, to having a healthy family, getting a seat on the bus to work or acing a work presentation. Now every time you're having a wobble or feeling a bit low you can take down your jar and read some of the great things in your life. It really will boost your amazing levels!

If a
CAULIFLOWER
can become a
PIZZA
BASE,
**then you can
become anything!**

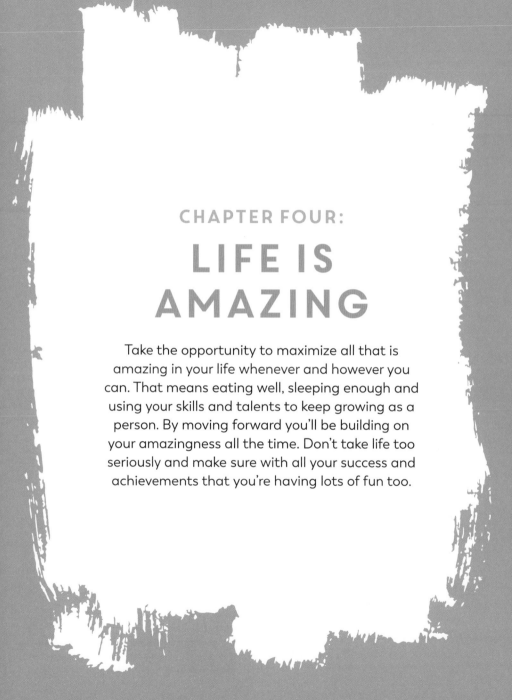

CHAPTER FOUR:

LIFE IS AMAZING

Take the opportunity to maximize all that is amazing in your life whenever and however you can. That means eating well, sleeping enough and using your skills and talents to keep growing as a person. By moving forward you'll be building on your amazingness all the time. Don't take life too seriously and make sure with all your success and achievements that you're having lots of fun too.

FILL YOUR PLATE WITH AMAZING FOOD

Think of your body as a finely tuned engine. If you don't put in good quality fuel, then you're not going to be operating at your most efficient levels. Try to eat whole foods where you can and avoid too many processed and packaged foods. Eat a rainbow of fruit and vegetables to ensure you're getting all the vitamins you need – or take a multivitamin if you need to. But don't forget to treat yourself to a slice of cake occasionally too! By eating a healthy balanced diet you'll have all the energy you need to get the most out of every day, leaving you full of beans to keep on being amazing.

I HAVE **ASPERGER'S** SYNDROME AND THAT MEANS I'M SOMETIMES A BIT **DIFFERENT** FROM THE NORM.

AND – GIVEN THE RIGHT CIRCUMSTANCES –

BEING DIFFERENT IS A SUPERPOWER.

GRETA THUNBERG

Don't be
afraid
to be
amazing

FIND YOUR PASSION

When life feels as though you're on a conveyer belt, it's hard to remember you once had dreams and passions. If family or work has taken over your life and your free time is non-existent, it is time to claw back your sense of self. If you were part of a band or choir when you were younger, find one to join now that you're an adult. Loved art classes at school? Try an evening class to reignite your passion. Did you use to play soccer or netball? Find a local club and join in. Remember what used to make you happy and actively seek it out.

STEP OUT OF YOUR SAFE ZONE

There is no point in never taking a chance in life just because you're scared. This year commit to challenging yourself in three different ways: mentally, physically and emotionally. Now you need to set your challenges. That might mean hiking to the top of a daunting mountain, combating your fear of spiders or learning to say no without the fear of offending others. Whatever you choose, write them down and put them somewhere you can see them, like the fridge door. Once you've achieved them, replace them with another challenge and keep on growing.

YOU ARE NEVER TOO OLD TO SET ANOTHER GOAL OR TO DREAM A NEW DREAM.

LES BROWN

GET MOVING

Endorphins – the feel-good chemicals that are released when you exercise – really do work. But you don't have to bounce out of bed to run 10 miles every morning or hike up a mountain. Instead choose something that works for you. Commit to a weekly dance class, try bouldering or take a daily stroll in your local park. Consistency is the key here so make sure you book in your activity with the same dedication as a doctor's appointment or work meeting. Set yourself a goal if you like – something simple like a "Couch to 5k" running app or a Fitbit to count you up to 10,000 steps is all it takes to see some real changes – in your mind and your body. The only thing that matters is that you enjoy what you're doing so you keep at it, ensuring you feel amazingly fit and healthy every day.

DO NOT COMPARE YOURSELF WITH STRANGERS ON THE INTERNET

SHARING IS CARING

When life feels less than amazing, it's easy to hunker down and wait for it to pass, but actually getting out there and giving some of your time is one of the fastest ways to feel better. Find a local charity that needs some help and commit some of your time. Maybe you can help sort donations one Saturday morning or perhaps they need a helpline to be covered for one night a week. You'll be amazed at all the inspirational people you meet and you'll quickly discover that you are one of those inspirational people too. It's win–win!

YOU CAN ALWAYS, ALWAYS
GIVE SOMETHING, EVEN IF
IT IS ONLY KINDNESS!

Anne Frank

LIFE
DOES
NOT
HAVE
TO BE
PERFECT
TO BE
WONDERFUL

> You can go as far as your mind lets you. What you believe, remember, you can achieve.

MARY KAY ASH

COOK UP A STORM

Learning to cook or expanding your repertoire is a great way to boost your health and happiness. Not only will you be able to make yourself nutritious food and save money on takeaways, but cooking is a great way to calm a busy mind and relax after a stressful day. Treat yourself to a new cookery book or try one of the recipe box services that can be delivered to your door. If you're really committed, try an evening class to teach you how to prepare some new dishes.

REACH FOR THE STARS

Nothing is out of reach, not even a trip to space if you dream hard enough. As proved by Jessica Meir, who was part of the first all-woman spacewalk alongside Christina Koch in October 2019. The astronaut, marine biologist and physiologist grew up gazing at the stars in rural Maine. She attributes her desire for space travel to her Swedish mother's love of nature and her Israeli father's sense of adventure. Jessica followed her passions despite having no real role models. She said: "There's no one path to becoming an astronaut. I think that's one of the great things about the job these days. You know, originally, all of the astronauts were white male military test pilots. And now the programme is much more diverse."

Your
only
limit
is your
own mind

WHEN WE STRIVE TO BECOME BETTER THAN WE ARE, EVERYTHING AROUND US BECOMES BETTER TOO.

Paulo Coelho

THE ONLY THING THAT STANDS IN THE WAY OF AN AMAZING LIFE

ARE THE EXCUSES YOU TELL YOURSELF AS TO WHY YOU CAN'T ACHIEVE IT

YOU'VE GOT THIS

You can handle anything life throws at you as long as you have the right attitude. If you view each up and down as an opportunity to learn and grow, you'll soon find that you are moving forward at a great pace in the direction that will lead you toward your goals. You are shaped by the things that happen to you in life, but you can decide if they knock you down or lift you up.

Don't ever make decisions based on fear. Make decisions based on hope and possibility.

Michelle Obama

SPARK SPONTANEITY

With every day of our week seemingly taken up with responsibilities such as work, grocery shopping and pre-arranged commitments, it can be hard to find any space to be spontaneous. Make a point of keeping one weekend a month unplanned and only decide your plans when you wake up on the day. Maybe you'll decide to pack a picnic and spend the day by the coast or you'll take a hike in a new area where you've never been before. Perhaps you'll treat yourself to a shopping trip and lunch at your favourite restaurant or you'll be free to accept a last-minute party invite. Whatever you decide you'll find that being unencumbered with plans will make your life feel lighter and open your mind to all the amazing things you could spend your time doing.

Don't
be
afraid
any more.
Not of
anyone
or anything.
Ever again.

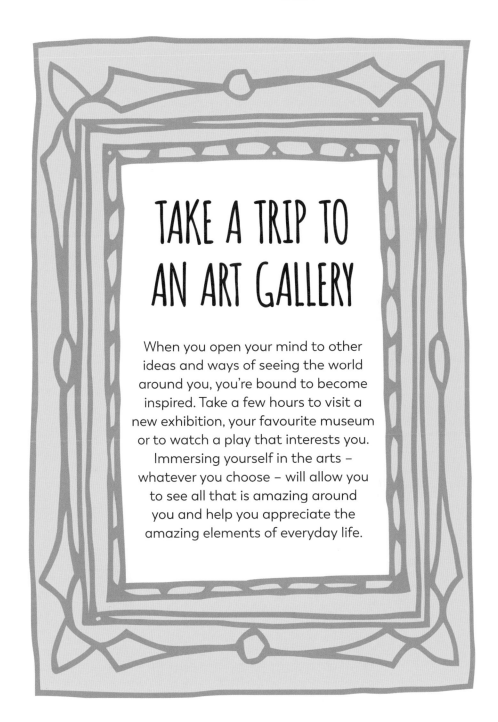

TAKE A TRIP TO AN ART GALLERY

When you open your mind to other ideas and ways of seeing the world around you, you're bound to become inspired. Take a few hours to visit a new exhibition, your favourite museum or to watch a play that interests you. Immersing yourself in the arts – whatever you choose – will allow you to see all that is amazing around you and help you appreciate the amazing elements of everyday life.

EMBRACE A NEW HOBBY

Take the plunge and take up a new hobby. The first step is giving something a go and enjoying trying something new, even if you're not very good at it. And you never know, you might discover a hidden skill or talent you never knew you had. But even if you don't, you'll meet interesting people and feel pretty amazing that you put yourself out there.

THIS IS YOUR MOMENT. OWN IT.

OPRAH WINFREY

YOU CAN ACHIEVE ANYTHING

There's a saying, "If you can't see it, then you can't be it". But Barack Obama didn't let that stop him when he started on his path to become America's first black president. He worked hard and inspired millions of people across the world. Whether or not you agree with his politics, no one can deny that he showed the world that anyone can do anything if they work hard enough. There's no goal too big if you truly want it. As Obama himself says: "It doesn't matter who you are or where you come from or what you look like... you can make it."

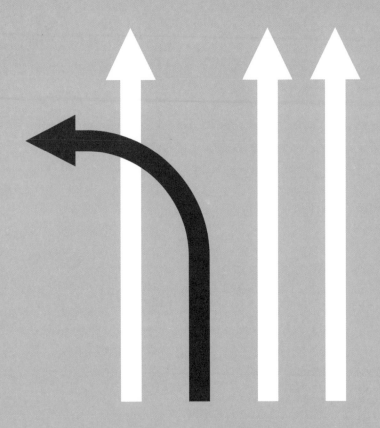

TURN OFF THE AUTOPILOT

It's all too easy to follow the next step in your education or career without stopping to think if this is really what you want. But it's never too late to put the brakes on and change direction. If you aren't happy with how your life is panning out, you have the power to change it. Simply by noticing you'd like to make a change you have taken the first step. Now you need to seize hold of the controls and start to live your life in the most amazing way you know how.

Go out
there
and be
amazing

CONCLUSION

By reading this book you should have realized how amazing you already are, but also that there's plenty you can do to ensure you are getting the maximum out of your life every day and also when it comes to bigger plans. Even the smallest step toward your goal is enough to get you going on the right track, although sometimes it will mean putting the brakes on and taking a U-turn. Make sure you live a life in line with your values and that you're happy with the direction in which you are going. Remember, no one is going to make your life amazing for you – it's up to you. So, take a chance and make a change; you'll be so pleased that you did.

IMAGE CREDITS

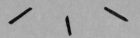

If you're interested in finding out
more about our books, find us on
Facebook at **Summersdale Publishers**
and follow us on Twitter at **@Summersdale**.

www.summersdale.com